A Heart Full of Prayer

Publications International, Ltd.

A Heart Full of Prayer

And all things, whatsoever ye shall ask in prayer, believing, ye shall receive.

—Matthew 21:22

We accept your invitation to pray without ceasing. Hear us as we pray boldly, with expectation, believing your assurance that we deserve to be in your presence and to talk all we want. We are grateful that you welcome us at all times and in all places and moods.

A Heart Full of Prayer

Morning Prayers

With wonder and trust, I greet you this morning, God of sunrise and rising dew. In gratitude, I look back to all that was good yesterday and in hope, face forward, ready for today.

My voice shalt thou hear in the morning, O Lord; in the morning will I direct my prayer unto thee, and will look up.

—Psalm 5:3

A Heart Full of Prayer

Good morning, God! We greet you with our many morning faces. We arise sometimes grumpy, sometimes smiling, sometimes prepared, sometimes behind. Always may we turn to you first in our family prayers. Bless us today and join us in it.

But I will sing of thy power; yea, I will sing aloud of thy mercy in the morning: for thou hast been my defence and refuge in the day of my trouble.

—Psalm 59:16

A Heart Full of Prayer

During the Day

God, help me celebrate this day with all my heart, to rejoice in the beauty of its light and warmth. May I give thanks for the air and grass and sidewalks. Help me feel grateful as I encounter others. May I cherish the chance to work and play, to think and speak—knowing this: All simple pleasures are opportunities for praise.

Rejoice in the Lord always: and again I say, Rejoice.

—Philippians 4:4

A Heart Full of Prayer

Lord, I've learned how to pray in strange but necessary places: in car pools, while cooking dinner, at the dentist, between loads of laundry, waiting in the checkout line. I've discovered that it's not how long I pray that matters but rather the very act of attempting to make a connection with you.

As for me, I will call upon God; and the Lord shall save me. Evening, and morning, and at noon, will I pray, and cry aloud: and he shall hear my voice.

—Psalm 55:16–17

A Heart Full of Prayer

Evening Praise

Alleluia, Lord! How we praise you with our words, our songs, and our lives! When we look back over all the situations you've brought us through, we are so grateful. We are filled with confidence that we can face the future because you will be there with us. And so we just want to stop today and praise you for all you are and all you do! Alleluia and Amen!

Let my prayer be set forth before thee as incense; and the lifting up of my hands as the evening sacrifice.

—Psalm 141:2

A Heart Full of Prayer

*L*ord, my heart overflows with gratitude for all the blessings you have sent into my life. I am cognizant of the fact that I am probably only aware of a small percentage of them, though. You are such a generous God; you shower us with such abundance. I am grateful for it all, Lord.

I am come that they might have life, and that they might have it more abundantly.

—John 10:10

A Heart Full of Prayer

During Difficult Times

Why can't we seem to get along, Lord? Is it me? For a few moments, I will just be silent…to listen for your answer.

O Lord never suffer us to think that we can stand by ourselves, and not need thee.

—John Donne

A Heart Full of Prayer

Dear God, you have sustained me through my illness. You have nursed my injury. You are my true physician, and I glorify you with all my heart.

When the darkness casts shadows upon us,

And the answers are nowhere in sight,

Hope lifts us up on a wing and a prayer

And carries us back to the light.

A Heart Full of Prayer

Seek the Lord

I come to church today, not because of duty or because a preacher calls, but because you, O God, invite me, your child, for whom you've been searching. In the words and songs, the lights and symbols, I feel, like a pulse, your spirit beating within me.

None but God can satisfy the longing of the immortal soul; as the heart was made for Him, He only can fill it.

—Richard Trench

A Heart Full of Prayer

May we rejoice in the written Word. The scriptures can come alive for us, if we only take, and read. Let us discover the acts of God in history, travel with his disciples along the pathway of service, and see how his church began and how it grew down through the centuries. Yes, let us celebrate the written Word, for it is a mirror of, and a witness to, the Living Word of the heavens.

How sweet are thy words unto my taste! yea, sweeter than honey to my mouth!

—Psalm 119:103

A Heart Full of Prayer

For Family

Bless mother and father, sister and brother, grandpa and grandma, uncle and aunt, and all the cousins. Here we are in your sight, this family: May we please you, day by day.

Thank you, God, for the gift of my sibling; for the bonds we share, the joys we experience, and the hardships we learn and grow from. We are blessed to have each other.

A Heart Full of Prayer

O God, instill in my children the heart of an adventurer off to explore every corner of your marvelous creation and to find their place in it. Thank you for blessing the quest and relieving my anxiety by promising to be a part of their journey step by step.

Keep thy father's commandment, and forsake not the law of thy mother.

—Proverbs 6:20

A Heart Full of Prayer

Thanks and Praise

Water that runs over moss-covered rocks: This is the sound of praise. Fingers that play upon ivory keys: This is the sound of worship. Silence that speaks even better than words: This is the sound of my thankful heart.

The pastures are clothed with flocks; the valleys also are covered over with corn; they shout for joy, they also sing.

—Psalm 65:13

A Heart Full of Prayer

Wonderful Words of Life

Christ, the blessed one, gives to all

Wonderful words of life;

Sinner heed now his loving call,

Wonderful words of life.

All so freely given,

Wooing us to heaven:

Beautiful words, wonderful words

Wonderful words of life.

—Phillip P. Bliss

A Heart Full of Prayer

Blessings at Meals

God, we thank you for this food,

For the hands that planted it,

For the hands that tended it,

For the hands that harvested it,

For the hands that prepared it,

For the hands that provided it,

And for the hands that served it.

And we pray for those without enough food

In your world and in our land of plenty.

A Heart Full of Prayer

He causeth the grass to grow for the cattle, and herb for the service of man: that he may bring forth food out of the earth.

—Psalm 104:14

Whether therefore ye eat, or drink, or whatsoever ye do, do all to the glory of God.

—1 Corinthians 10:31

Lord of Dreams and Journeys

I always want to be a dreamer, O God, to feel the stir and the yearning to see my vision become reality. There are those who would say dreamers are free-floaters. When I dream I feel connected to you and to your creation, bound by purpose and a sense of call. Nourish my dreams and my striving to make them real.

I press toward the mark for the prize of the high calling of God in Christ Jesus.

—Philippians 3:14

A Heart Full of Prayer

Our Earth

Bless the soil beneath our feet, the sky overhead, and make us one with it. We are catching on, catching up with ourselves, creator God, and catching a whiff of the garbage we're burying ourselves beneath. Catching, too, a glimpse of the fading streams and trash-strewn seas we have long ignored.

Bless and use our reclamation efforts, for it is a task we can't accomplish alone. With your help, we can bind up and reclaim this poor old earth. We feel whispers of hope in the winds of changed hearts and minds, for we recall your promise to make all things new—even this earth we shall yet learn to tend. We are grateful for another chance.

God's Love

I t's hard, Lord, to reveal my heart to you, though it's the thing I most want to do. Remind me in this dialogue that you already know what is within me. You wait—O thank you!—hoping for the gift of my willingness to acknowledge the good you already see and the bad you've long forgotten.

To be in Christ is the source of the Christian's life; to be like Christ is the sum of His excellence; to be with Christ is the fullness of his joy.

—Charles Hodge

Heart Full of Prayer

$\mathcal{L}$ord, many times I have asked you to protect my heart from wanton wanderings, and you have always aided me. How grateful I am for your help, Lord. Thank you for steering my heart toward only what is good and true. My heart is full of love for many people, but it only belongs to you.

$\mathcal{G}$od wants us to love him, not because he is greedy for love, but because when we are devoted to loving him, we get in touch with his powerful, everlasting love for us. When we do, we cannot contain it, and it overflows to others.

A Heart Full of Thanks

Lord, you are the God who has set the foundations of the earth, who blessed Abraham with offspring "as numerous as the stars in heaven." You have blessed me, too, by giving me the treasure of my heart, my family. I pour out my thanks for these gifts, which are far above any riches the world can give. How can I praise you enough?

You bring beauty, peace, and love to my existence. My heart overflows with thanksgiving.

A Heart Full of Prayer

Heavenly Father, I never fail to come to you for help and comfort in the dark times of my life, yet I don't always remember you when my cup is overflowing. Forgive me if I seem ungrateful and take your generosity for granted. How can I forget all that you give me each day?

To the end that my glory may sing praise to thee, and not be silent. O Lord my God, I will give thanks unto thee for ever.

—Psalm 30:12

A Heart Full of Prayer

God's Faithfulness

When I think about your faithfulness to me, Lord, my heart overflows! I long to share this treasure trove with the people around me. When I consider all that you have done for me, I am overwhelmed by your love.

Thy mercy, O Lord, is in the heavens; and thy faithfulness reacheth unto the clouds.

—Psalm 36:5

A Heart Full of Prayer

There are many aspects of life that are easy to take for granted: the air that I breathe, the rain for the crops, the food that I eat, and the relationships that I have. I sometimes forget how blessed I am. I want to take time every day to really contemplate how faithfully you work in my life. Once all of your blessings are fresh in my mind, it will be impossible to hide my gratitude. Your faithfulness will be on the tip of my tongue and in the innermost recesses of my heart.

O Lord, thou art my God; I will exalt thee, I will praise thy name; for thou hast done wonderful things; thy counsels of old are faithfulness and truth.

—Isaiah 25:1

A Simple Prayer

O Lord, please help me to understand that I won't always get what I pray for. In the same regard, I want to learn to thank you more for everything you do give me. Amen.

S peak, move, act in peace, as if you were in prayer. In truth, this is prayer.

—Francois de Salignace
de La Mothe Fenelon